ENCOMPASS

Three Plays by

Roger Goldsmith and Janet Rawson

Published by Playdead Press 2023

© Roger Goldsmith & Janet Rawson

Roger Goldsmith and Janet Rawson have asserted their rights under the Copyright, Design and Patents Act, 1988, to be identified as the author of this work.

A CIP catalogue record for this book is available from the British Library.

ISBN 978-1-915533-20-3

Caution

All rights whatsoever in this play are strictly reserved and application for performance should be sought through the author before rehearsals begin. No performance may be given unless a license has been obtained.

This book is sold subject to the condition that it shall not by way of trade or otherwise, be lent, resold, hired out, or otherwise circulated without the publisher's prior consent in any form of binding or cover other than that in which it is published and without a similar condition including this condition being imposed on the subsequent purchaser.

Playdead Press
www.playdeadpress.com

Encompass was first performed at Groundings Theatre, Portsmouth on Wednesday 1st November 2023 with the following cast:

The Deserter

JACK SMITH | **Joseph Scatley**

Written by Roger Goldsmith
Directed by April Singley

Birth

CYBIL | **April Singley**

Written by Roger Goldsmith
Directed by Joseph Scatley

2049 AD

MADAME MEDUSA | **April Singley**

DEREK | **Joseph Scatley**

Written and directed by Janet Rawson

CAST

April Singley
April trained at the Royal Birmingham Conservatoire, obtaining her MFA in Acting after more than a decade of film and theatre work. April has appeared in many Shakespeare productions in the UK and USA.

Joseph Scatley
Joseph trained at Rose Bruford College, where he received an MA in Actor Performer Training. He has been performing since he was a child, working with the BBC, ITV, The National Theatre and Shakespeare's Globe Theatre.

CREATIVE

Janet Rawson
Janet's play *Thrilling* played at the Edinburgh Fringe and The Man in the Moon, London. *Mopsy, Flopsy and Death* at The Hen and Chickens, London, and was translated and published in German and premiered in Vienna.

Roger Goldsmith
Roger's *It Started With A Touch* played at Wimbledon Studios and Barons Court Theatre. *Runaway* by Small But Mighty Theatre in Toronto. *Freehold* was produced by Barons Court Theatre

CONTENTS

THE DESERTER | page 7

BIRTH | page 25

2049 AD | page 39

THE DESERTER

by

ROGER GOLDSMITH

CHARACTERS

JACK SMITH | *Mid twenties*

A house somewhere in London, in 1919

Sound of the First World War song 'It's A Long Way to Tipperary'.

JACK SMITH *slumped in an armchair. He wears blue striped pyjamas, carpet slippers. Fair hair. London Cockney accent. Youthful, almost boyish looking. It's the middle of the night. He looks exhausted. The music stops.*

JACK: (*rubs his eyes*) Can't sleep. When did I have a proper sleep? Like when? Can't remember. Sodden dreams. (*looks at his watch*) What time is it? Half past three.

Gotta be out the house in three hours. Get the key from Mrs Spencer before she goes to the factory. Make a start stripping her dining room walls. She'll give me an earful and more besides if I'm not there on time. I know what she's like.

He takes a photo out of his pyjama pocket.

She always looks the same in my dreams. Me ten. And her... I don't know how old... Young. And beautiful. Everyone said how beautiful she was.

Mr Hardcastle in the fruit and vegetable shop. How's your Mum today, Jack?

Give her my regards. (*knowingly, off*) Yeah, and more besides.

And Mr Lawrence, the butcher. He was always saying nice things about her. (*imitates*) Mr

> Hardcastle said to give you these strawberries as a present Mum. You said a quarter of mince, but Mr Lawrence said he put in six ounces as a little something extra.
>
> Mr Lawrence with his rosy cheeks. He was always laughing. It must be working in a butchers does it. I've heard that. Working with meat makes you happy.

He runs his fingers though his hair. Tries to reason. Gesticulates

> The dreams are like, mixed up. It's not like… One scene. I don't just see them. As they were. Him and her. Together. It's jumbled up. Like… like dreams are, I suppose.
>
> I look through the keyhole and see her pleading with him. Crying. 'Don't leave me, please don't leave me.' I look behind me, and see a line of men, one after the other, on the landing, on the stairs, out the front door. Like conscription. Like when I joined the army. Speeded up. Like a Harold Lloyd film.
>
> I wake up, and hear the ticking of the clock. Back to real again.
>
> People knocking on the door for money. Threatening her. Threatening us. Working as a cleaner scrubbing floors at the school wasn't gonna pay back all his debts. What *else* was she to do? (*imitates*) You're his wife, his debts are your debts.
>
> We want our money. Or else.

She was scared. Scared for me. Scared for both of us.

She always bought me a quarter of Liquorice Allsorts when she had a man in the house, and said for me to stay in the lounge. When someone knocked on the front door she'd give me a great big hug and told me how much she loved me before she answered it. And when they'd gone she'd do the same.

(*darkly*) Once, I heard one of them shouting abuse at her, calling her a slag. He was drunk and fat and bloated, and sweating. I punched and kicked him. Leave my Mum alone, I said. Leave her alone!

I banged and kicked on her bedroom door, and asked her if she was all right. And she said she was, and not to worry, softly like a little bird who'd broken its wing.

She always tried to be my Mum. Proper. Like Mums are supposed to be.

I always told her what Mr Hardcastle and Mr Lawrence said when she was sitting on the bed looking worried and upset, and needed cheering up. I'd hold her hands and kiss them, front and back, I'd entwine my fingers in hers, and hold them tight.

And when she said, come on Jack, I've got things to do, let me get up, I'd hold her there, for a few more minutes, straighten the cross on the chain round neck, pull on her pinafore belt and make reef knots just to keep being close because I loved her so much.

He holds the photo at arm's length with one hand.

I thought she might do something stupid. Take an overdose or something, cos it all got too much for her. But no. She died of a broken heart. That's what the doctor said. Your Mother died of a broken heart, Jack.

I never believed people could die of a broken heart. (*hand under his heart*) A heart in here breaking in two. Like. In two bits. I'd need to see it. For real. I never believed what I couldn't see. Like God. But no. She died of a broken heart cos of him leaving her.

And the letters. The letters she wrote and never sent. To tell him how much she loved him. Why did she write them? What was the point of it? He was gone.

She'd never see him again. It was bloody madness. But she wasn't mad. She was a dreamer. She dreamed he'd come back. And even if he didn't, it didn't matter.

I forgive you, she wrote. On every letter. At the end of every one. I love you and I forgive you.

Jack stands.

When the blokes in the trenches got letters from home, I'd sit and look at their faces. One by one. A line of them. Watching their reactions. Quiet. Like the grave.

And then… sudden laughter. Sadness sometimes, if something bad happened back home. But mostly laughter.

And for days afterwards they'd be happy. The letters lifted them. Made them forget what a shit hole they were in and likely to die at any time, and never see home again. Not dressed in uniforms, with helmets, carrying useless fucking rifles and bayonets. But home. Where they belonged.

Haven't you got any letters Jack? No, I haven't What about a girlfriend? Haven't got one. Your Mum and Dad then? My Mum's dead. And my Dad ran off when I was ten.

(*upstanding, formally*) I was twenty two. Painter and decorated in civvy street. Private Jack Smith in the army. Better at wallpapering and especially long drops in civvy street. Better at nothing in the army. Good at gloss painting and window frames, and doors in civvy street. Better at nothing in the army. I didn't wanna be there anyway. Who did?

I was thinking of my Mum's porridge and golden syrup spread all over it, when I heard a call.

We've found someone in the barn!

We've found a deserter!

I pulled my rifle back, pointed it at his head. What are you doing, a soldier said?

You can't shoot him. He's gotta have a court martial. A trial.

I wanted to kill him. There and then. No need for a court martial. No need for a trial. He was guilty. On all counts. When you wanna do something just do it.

Don't think. Never think. Thinking fucks up your instincts and my instincts were to blow his fucking brains out. I would've and all if no one was around.

Commanding officer Rattigan. Rat face they called him. On account of him looking like a rat. He made me stand to attention for fifteen minutes at least.

He wrote this letter with a fountain pen, and kept on stopping to think, and looked up at me, as if he expected me to tell him what to write or something. A sergeant brought him some tea and he drank it slowly.

What's the meaning of your behaviour, Private Smith? I said I was sorry.

Sorry? You could be court martialled for that, do you realise that? I said I was sorry. Sorry. I should hope you are bloody sorry. I said I was.

I couldn't stop myself. It was like floodgates opening. (*fiercely*) I wanna be in the firing squad, sir. I'm volunteering right now. I told him how much I hated fucking deserters. People who ran out on things. Fighting for King and Country.

Preserving the British Empire. Upholding the union jack. Guarding our shores. Loyalty. Dedication to duty. That's what counts. That's *all* that counts.

He said that was commendable. I said I know. He said don't swear. I said I won't no more sir.

Jack moves to a different place.

Two of them dragged him to the same barn they found him in for the court martial.

His feet got stuck in the mud. And they hit him with the butt of their rifles. They hit him a lot. And he bled. He bled a lot.

After ten minutes Rat face came out. He lit a cigarette. What's the verdict sir? I said to him. Once we have Field Marshall Douglas Haig's approval he'll be shot at dawn.

Same as before. I was burning up. (*fiercely*) I want a rifle with a live bullet in it, sir. I don't want one with a blank in. I wanna know I killed him. Deserting bastard.

I wanna know it was me who did it. I wanna be the one.

Rat face looked at me, curious like. Private Smith, are you sure you don't know this man? And don't have a personal vendetta against him?

I said I'd never seen him in my life. And I didn't know what a personal vendetta was.

Silence.

Ants ran all over me. I was hungry. I wanted porridge. I wanted my Mum. I wanted a hot bath and soak for hours. I wanted the warmth of a blanket wrapped around my body and a water bottle warming my feet and my Mum tucking me in, to take away every bad feeling I had.

It was just gone half past three. I couldn't sleep. I tossed and turned thinking about it. I couldn't wait till dawn. I wanted to be out there now, waiting for them to bring him.

This corporal kicked me, woke me up, just as I was nodding off.

Private Smith. He wants to see you. Who? I said. The prisoner, of course. Who else? What for? I said. How the bloody hell should I know? he said. Come on, get a move on.

Two guards were smoking, showing photos to each other, smiling, and he was there, in the wet straw.

The place smelt of shit. Not cow's shit. I know what cow's shit smells like. I spent a month on this farm in Devon with an aunt and her two boys. It smells milky. I don't know what shit it was. Human shit probably. His.

He didn't notice me at first. He was reading this small book, turned out to be a Bible, cupped in his hands, like cupping water from a fountain. His hair was jet black, there was mud in it, and his dark thick eyebrows looked just the same.

What do you want? I said.

He lowered this, this small Bible, in his lap, and just looked at me. I got nervous. Twitchy. My heart was pounding.

The two guards were laughing their heads off at something, and I wondered what they were laughing at. Were they laughing at me, standing there saying nothing like an idiot?

I felt like I did when I pissed myself in class sometimes or when my tummy rumbled, when I was asked a question and I didn't know the answer, and I just wanted to run and run and run and not be there. The silence was unbearable. It was too bloody much. My mouth went dry, and I couldn't swallow. I thought I was gonna suffocate.

YOU'RE GONNA DIE TOMORROW YOU BLOODY COWARD.

Both guards stood up. One of them told me to shut it or piss off. They backed off looking at me all the time. You've got five minutes, one of them said.

He was calm. He breathed slow. His eyes didn't bulge and the muscles in his neck and the veins... they never showed. Not like before. He had a smile. Like he was at peace.

Sorry if I woke you up Jack, but I wanted to tell you something. Something important...

There *was* someone else, Jack. Another woman. Someone I met two years before I left you and your Mum.

What was wrong with my Mum? I said. She was beautiful. Mr Lawrence and Mr Hardcastle both said so. Everyone said so.

I'm sorry, but these things happen in life, son. They do. You'll find out yourself one day. It was the first time I ever remember him calling me son.

Her name was Mary. Mary got ill. Very ill. I needed money to pay for treatment. I started gambling. And drinking. I couldn't stop gambling. I couldn't stop drinking. It became an obsession. Took over my life. Took over everything.

Then Mary died. A slow, painful, horrible death. It destroyed me. I didn't want to go on. I wanted to kill myself. I didn't want to be here anymore.

Then God came into my life. And he changed me. I gave my life to God. And he saved me. I joined the Ministry. I deserted my regiment, because I wanted to go back home and help people, in my community. Pray with them. Pray for them. Comfort them. Be there for them.

I never wanted to fight. It was against all I stood for. I thought I'd got it wrong. I prayed and prayed. And still the same answer. Volunteer. Join up. And now I know why. It was to meet you Jack.

That's bollocks.

Me to see you. You to see me.

That's shit. The way you're shit.

It was fate, he said.

I don't believe in fate. It's all shit.

It's God's plan for us, he said.

(*angrily*) God doesn't exist. Cos if he does, why would he let all these people die? What sort of plan is that? Why is there a war? What's it all for? What's the point of it? All those dead soldiers. Young kids. Boys of sixteen, seventeen slaughtered. Like pigs. If there's a God why don't he do something about it?

I've made my peace with God. Now I want to make my peace with with you, Jack. Please forgive me for what I did. To you and your Mum.

No. I don't forgive you. I'll never forgive you. You bastard. One of the soldiers called out... You've got two minutes Smith.

God Bless you Jack. Peace be with you.

He lowered his head, and pulled the Bible in front of him, in his lap, and started reading.

I wanted to tell him we was all right. He'd deserted her, he'd deserted me, but we was all right, both of us. She was alive and kicking and happy with me looking after her, working as a painter decorator, supporting her, looking after her. I opened my mouth, but nothing came out. I couldn't speak. I couldn't move. Like a statue. A dumb bloody statue. I couldn't say anything. I couldn't say a thing.

Not a bloody thing.

>Time's up Smith, the solider said. Out you go. Get some sleep, son. You'll need all the sleep you can get. We're going over the top tomorrow.

Silence.

>I dreamt of him telling me about The Arsenal. How he went to watch them with his Dad. With this wooden rattle. It made so much bloody noise. (*imitates*) I'll take you one day to see The Arsenal. Just like my Dad did. He never did though.

Silence.

>A soldier kicked me. Private Smith. Wake up. Got shooting practice, son. You'll like that, won't you?
>
>I wanted to be first out there. But I was last. I was so tired. Rat face was there. And the other five. All holding their rifles.
>
>You're late Smith, Rat face said. Come on, line up with the others. We want to get this over with.
>
>The same corporal who woke me in the night threw me a rifle. I was in a daze. Half asleep.
>
>I looked at the Enfield like I'd never seen one before.
>
>Rat face walked up to me. Come on Private Smith. Where's all that fire in your belly gone, son? Ah? You don't seem up for it.
>
>Pull yourself together. Get moving.
>
>Line up with the others.

I stood on the end. The soldier cleaning his boots stood beside me. He smelt of cigarette and shit.

Perhaps it was him who shit in the barn.

He was stood by this tree. It was bare. It looked dead. Like a skeleton. It was a grey morning. Almost dark.

There was a white sheet pinned to his chest, with a red cross painted on it.

I wondered about his eyes. If I'd see them when I fired. If we'd look at each other.

But he was blindfolded.

I did what they did. I lifted my rifle. I was last. It all happened so quickly. Rat face gave the order. FIRE.

He fell to the ground. The other soldiers walked away. No one said anything. It was just me and Rat face.

A soldier appeared out of no where and bent down to him. Took off his blindfold.

He's not dead. He's still breathing.

Rat face looked at me, with this smirk on his face.

You heard what the soldier said, he's not dead Private Smith. He took out this pistol. Let's see that fire in your belly.

I shook my head. I can't. I can't do it sir.

It's an order, Private Smith. I'm giving you an order. Shoot him!

I took the gun from him, and looked at it. I wanted to ask him if it was me who fired the blank. But I didn't. I just kept looking at the gun.

(*imitates, loudly*) Hurry up Private Smith, before I charge you with disobeying a commanding officer!

I stood over him. The white sheet was... full of blood, smudged, like a child's, like a child's first go at painting, paint all over the place. His eyes were closed, and his eyelids were flickering, as if he... And blood poured out his mouth.

I heard Rat face's boots squelch in the mud and felt his hot breath on my neck.

Right Private Smith, if you're not man enough to do it, I will. He grabbed the pistol out of my hand and shot him between the eyes.

He takes hold of the photo again. Kisses it. Faces.

There was a smile on his face. Like when we played football. He'd throw the ball high up in the air, and the ball got lost in the bright sunshine, and he closed his eyes as he waited for it to come down and hit him on the head. I remembered that moment. Just for a second.

Silence.

I only said it cos of her, cos I loved her, cos of my love for her, and it's what she'd want. It's shit I know,

> I have dreams about it, nightmares, I wake up thinking about it… but I swear there was a flicker of his eyebrows when I said it, as if, as if he heard. Cos it would be no good, it wouldn't work, none of it, if he didn't hear, if he was dead before I said it.
>
> Would it? I mean would it?
>
> I forgive you Dad.
>
> Not that I believe it. Not that I believe any of it. It's bollocks. It's all a load of shit really.

Jack smiles.

> He'd be pleased about The Arsenal. They'll be playing in League Division 1 next season. Football league's taking two teams from Division 2 to make twenty two teams in Division one. And The Arsenal are one of them.
>
> I've still got his wooden rattle. I'll have to go and see The Arsenal sometime.
>
> Rattle it as loud as I can. Drive everyone around me bloody mad.

Silence.

> Three hundred and six of them were shot. Deserters I mean.
>
> I wonder if he knew… About her being dead.

Blackout

End of Play

BIRTH

by
ROGER GOLDSMITH

CHARACTERS

CYBIL | *late thirties*

A dining room somewhere in the London suburbs.

The sound of 'Jerusalem' plays.

A pine table, Centre.

CYBIL *sits at the table, writing a letter, using a fountain pen. She wears glasses and has short hair. She wears conservative clothes, a tweed skirt and blouse. The music stops.*

CYBIL: I think that will do.

She puts the letter in an envelope and seals it.

> I never know what to say. But he does say it doesn't matter what you write, just write... So I do.

She puts a stamp on the letter. She looks at the letter. She takes off her glasses, puts them on the table.

> He says he's sorry every time I go. After which he sits there saying very little. I get embarrassed because when I say things I'm not sure he listens, and he only sees me because he feels guilty and thinks he should.

She stands.

> When I leave he says, you *will* come and see me next week, won't you? And I say, yes, I will.

She walks to the side. Looks down. Smiles.

Rose. My beautiful Rose. Fast asleep and dreaming of green, green, grass and rolling English countryside, I've no doubt.

Looks down. Smiles.

I do love you my beautiful Queen bee. You are the joy of my life. And more. So much more.

Father, of course, were he alive, would frown on the whole thing. (*smiles*) Mother, too. But they're both dead. So they cannot say a thing. Although sometimes I dream they are alive. I wake up in a cold sweat and see them in my mind's eye, standing at the foot of the bed, Father putting on his dog collar, smelling of Old Spice and Mother with her rubber gloves and secateurs that look, in the dream or the aftermath of it, somewhat menacing. As though they were intended for something other than cutting back the roses.

But they are both dead. That is a fact. They won't come back... Ever.

Silence.

I feel blessed. I *do* feel blessed. Should I thank God for her? Is there a God? I grew up having God pummelled into me so much he became an invisible guest at breakfast lunch and supper. He would not go away. And I wished he would.

There was a place for him at the table. Always. He was referred to, quoted, revered, loved, acknowledged.

Oh how I longed to be wild, released from the chains of a Mother and Father whose devotion to God seemed, in many ways, unnatural. (*reconsiders*) No. Not it seemed. Not in many ways. It *was* unnatural. I was never quoted, listened to, loved. Not in the way love should be. Not in the way I needed!

They'd taken off in their prized Morris Minor for Oxford for the day to see aunt Mabel. When I came back from the library, and there was a police car outside of the house, I knew they were both dead. A moustached policeman broke the news to me. And I pictured them, the turtle waxed shiny black of the bonnet crumpled, and the two of them with their heads through the windscreen, horribly disfigured, and quite unrecognisable as my Mother and Father. The Mother and Father I knew.

Father always said articulated vehicles were dangerous. And how profound his comment turned out to be. I say it now because it's true, and if there is a God and he is my witness, and judges me, as I have always been taught he judges us all, I will never see him, because I smiled and felt a tremendous sense of relief.

God had overstayed his welcome. And so had they.

I remember saying to the two policeman, quite brightly. (*animated*) Would you like a cup of tea, and some chocolate digestive biscuits?

They looked at me, somewhat surprised. I cottoned on pretty quickly, and matched the severity of the situation with a suitably stark look of deep regret and shock and horror, which seemed to settle things down and hold it at the level befitting of such an announcement. Level footing again. English playing fields.

(*recites*) And did those feet in ancient time Walk upon England's mountains green...

Father began every day before breakfast standing on the veranda singing the first four verses of Jerusalem. It seemed appropriate, therefore, for the church choir to bow him out in the same way.

Mother too. One coffin after the other. The curtains closing on them in the same way Mother closed the lounge curtains at dusk.

Silence.

I longed for sex from a very early age. I think Mother knew how much I masturbated, because often, after dinner, and sometimes before, when I was fifteen, and younger, she would look at me reading the works of Chaucer, in Father's words 'the Father of English poetry', which I always hated, but read because Father thought it was becoming of me, and concentrate a look... (*she flaps a finger at herself*) ...down here. And she would say, are you all right, Cybil, is everything in order? And I would say, yes, the Chaucer is wonderful. What a writer. What a man. Such wisdom. Those wonderful quotations. And she said that's not what I meant, Cybil. Your privates. Is everything in order with your privates? Your lower regions?

She always topped off the inquiry, which was always matter of fact and perfunctory with the dramatically toned...' Remember. Pure thoughts, Cybil. Pure thoughts. God is watching you.' (*knowingly*) She knew. I know she did.

Mother and Father made it abundantly clear, that after they had done it, and I was conceived, that was it. Sex was out. For good. It was history. It did not exist. It had served its purpose for the function of creating me, and as such was not acknowledged further as being desirable or necessary. Not like God. The constant guest.

And reading three verses of the King James Bible every day, and eating a balanced diet and getting eight hours sleep a night and polishing one's leather shoes daily was far more necessary. The primary function. The English way.

Fanny. It's still hard for me to say the word fanny with any modicum of comfort... Fanny. Fanny. Fanny.

(*smiles nervously, enjoying the indulgence*) I have a red hot fanny. I have a scorching fanny. My fanny is so hot that... I have a cat on a hot tin roof fanny.

Burning like only a cat on a hot tin roof fanny can.

(*remembers*) Church. Fourteen years of age. David Hopkins. Fifteen years of age. I always sat next to him. As close as I could. Our legs touching. My thoughts racing. In prayer my lowered head would wander from thanks to God on high, to the lump in David Hopkins' trousers below.

But nothing happened. Nothing was ever going to happen. I was going to die not only of being a virgin, but of never being loved. The emptiness of death. That solitude. That nothingness. That void. The black. That silence.

She looks at her watch.

(*looking towards Rose*) He'll be here soon, won't he, my beautiful Rose? He's very prompt.

She draws her eyes away slowly. Faces.

The last book I stamped before I closed the library, and left for the mile walk home was Lawrence's Lady Chatterley's lover. I remembered aunt Florence telling me how she read it, guiltily, when she was a young girl, how she spilt tea on it with sheer excitement as she turned the pages to the 'best bits' as she called them. How she rubbed the tea stains with a cloth and rubbed so hard she made holes in the pages. I'm sure I was thinking of aunt Florence when it happened.

They asked him in court why he did it. Darren. That's his name.

Darren had an argument with his girlfriend, Zena, a nurse from South Africa.

She'd found someone else, and had broken off her engagement with him. He was angry and upset. He felt the need to take his anger and aggression out on someone.

And that someone was me.

As I walked passed the mouth of the alleyway, leading to the market, he promptly dragged me into a recess of the rear of a vegetable shop, unseen by passers by, pulled me down, and raped me.

In court he said he was drunk, and didn't know what he was doing.

If he were not drunk would he have chosen someone other than me to vent his feelings on? Whilst I was pure, so called, and totally inexperienced, I did get looks from men, occasionally. Mainly older men I confess, balding and toothless, but that did at least constitute some recognition of the fact that I was a woman, and had things to offer.

The judge seemed slightly perturbed by my reaction when I said he wasn't drunk, and I was careful not to enlarge on it, for fear of more searching questions, such as, did you let him, did you enjoy it, did you try to stop him? All of which I would naturally have answered in the negative to. Obviously... Obviously.

In my defence, or his, he did say he had no intention of hurting me. And for some inexplicable reason, I believed him. Why, I have no idea.

Silence.

The second he orgasmed I knew I was pregnant. He got off me, stood up, put his thing away, pulled up his pants and trousers, did up his zip, tightened his belt, and left. I lay in silence for several seconds as I heard the pounding of his feet on the pavement.

I ask myself to this day, if I had not been seen, pulling up my knickers and pulling down my skirt, and he had not been seen running away, stopped in his tracks by two testosterone-filled weightlifters on their way to a gym in the alleyway, would we have ever come to face each other again? And I could have had my baby under totally different circumstances.

Silence.

The irony of it. Sympathy. In abundance. Such an outpouring. The family, such as it was left, the dying breed, rallied round, took turns to come and visit me. The Vicar. Vicar Carson. The congregation. The house was always full. It was like a never ending wake.

Never in my thirty eight years had I been bestowed with so much... thought. I lived. I existed. I wasn't someone who people nodded to in the street, smiled emptily and shook hands with after church, someone who aunts and uncles referred to as 'and family' on Christmas greetings cards. Not some afterthought. I was real. I was a person. In my own right.

I loved it. I acted. I playacted and wondered why I had never playacted before. I was actually quite good at it. At the beginning of every day, with my schedule of visitors and the times of their arrival established, I looked in the mirror, and prepared for the onslaught. Prepared to be wounded, destroyed, devastated, heartbroken, suicidal.

The local medical centre sent a stream of various doctors to attend to me.

Medication was offered. The societies. Organizations I did not know existed knocked reverently on my door, and treated me oh so gently, and carefully, and with such sensitivity.

On one occasion a doctor I had not seen before appeared. He looked like a film star. Or someone with his looks who should be in films. Wonderful blue eyes. Jet black hair. Mid thirties. Athletic. I immediately went into overdrive. And raised the level of my performance several notches higher in order to evoke as much sympathy as I possibly could. We sat on Father's favourite sofa. We sat on Father's favourite sofa, beige and very stained from thirty years of use, but it was from Harrods, so it always remained.

I managed tears. Lots of them. I put my hand on his knee, the way I had always wanted to put my hand on David Hopkins' knee and beyond. Quite justified.

Never a hint of anything but natural reactions. He held my hand, and said, time is a great healer Cybil. And I said, yes, it is, you are *so, so right* Doctor. I was in a haze of disbelief. A place I had never ever been before. This was heaven. This was the real heaven. This would do. This I could take. This I wanted more of.

He left me his card with his home number on and said ring me, if there is anything else I can do for you. My thoughts ran wild. I *was* wild. Crazy. I'd been raped and I was pregnant by my attacker and I was the happiest I had ever been in my entire life. And here I was with the handsomest doctor in England asking me if there was anything he could do and to ring him at any time, day or night!

When the door closed on the last visitor for the day, and they'd all gone, I sighed with relief, took off my mask, and danced for joy, the way I'm sure I danced when I was a very young girl but could not remember. I hopped and skipped up the stairs, and sang the way I had never ever sung. I stripped off my clothes and ran around the house naked. Joy in abundance. Happiness in abundance.

They all said, the family, the dying breed, the people whose opinions mattered, that I should have an abortion. Just imagine what it will look like. Turn out like.

I said I'll have you know Darren's quite good looking actually, even by my lowest of low standards. And he runs a perfectly well respected Kebab take-away. In fact he won a prize last year for the best Kebab take-away in town. He has a rosette to prove it.

What more can a woman want than a baby fathered by a man with such culinary talents?

The knowing looks to each other, the nothing said, the asides, the deep breaths, the air of resignation. (*imitates*) A gentle hug and a splattering of suitably softly spoken 'take cares' and they were gone.

Smiles more.

And of course, the saving Grace of it all, the what goes round comes around, the icing on the cake bit, was, paradoxically – though paradoxically is probably not the right word, in this context – was Mother and Father, dear Mother and Father's devotion to Him on high. And the wonder of the King James bible with its abundance of books and verses and lines of comfort and support. God is love.

Forgiveness is all.

I went through the Bible, selecting suitable sections to quote to anyone who annoyingly never missed a Sunday service and who dared to criticise me. I pinned them on Father's study wall and with a discipline he would commend and be proud of me for, learned them, one by one, in readiness for their opposition.

Matthew 6. Verses 14 and 15. Quote. 'For if you forgive men when they sin against you, your heavenly Father will also forgive you, But if you do not forgive men their sins, your Father will not forgive your sins.' Unquote. And all the others, too numerous to mention. But consistent in their divine philosophies.

Aunt Winifred said, you can't call her Rose, when she first laid eyes on her in hospital. She's black. What would your Mother and Father say if you saw that you'd given birth to a black child?

I said, well, Darren is black, what colour do you expect her to be? I duly reminded her that on the Sunday sermon before Father's untimely death he quoted from Doctor Martin Luther King's famous 'I have a dream' speech. She said, oh did he?

I said yes he did.

Two rings of the doorbell, a moment, and then a third.

That's him. Michael. Michael works in the library. Michael has his own key. He always has a shower, and puts on a silk dressing gown I bought him. He sits in the study at Father's desk, until I tell him I'm ready for him.

I lay one of Father's favourite Persian rugs in front of the table, so I can see Rose as we are having sex. I want her to be aware. From an early age. Of everything.

She adjusts an imaginary picture on the wall.

Mother and Father, too. I like them looking down on me.

I still work in the library. Part-time. Two days a week. Though I'm not in charge of it now, of course. I have a childminder. Agnes. From Poland.

Michael's twenty one. He's very quiet. We never talk in the library. We never talk here. We turn over pages. He turns over me.

She takes off her blouse and her skirt as she says the following.

When I went to the prison last week, I showed Darren a photo of Rose. For the first time. He'd never asked to see one before. She's very beautiful, he said. She has my exact colouring. I said, she is from you, Darren, what do you expect?

Darren smiled. I smiled.

Aunt Winifred came to mind. And Mother and Father, too. I've found the love I wanted. I feel complete. I want for nothing. Perhaps there is a God after all.

She leaves.

Blackout

End of Play

2049 AD

by

JANET RAWSON

CHARACTERS

MADAME MEDUSA | *A woman of indeterminate age, Interviewer for Central.*

CRACK | *An extremely camp Security Guard, unseen.*

DEREK | *An interviewee applying to Central. He thinks he is God's gift to women. In his late 20s.*

The action takes place in one stark, unadorned room, that has one table and two chairs.

The stage is in darkness. A stark light is suddenly snapped on. It hangs over a table in the centre of the room with two chairs either side of it. It also reveals **MADAME MEDUSA.**

She is apparently dozing with her feet up on the table in front of her. She is in a severe but sexy uniform that emphasises the female figure. Her hair is pulled up very high into a pony-tail at the top of her head. This has the effect of pulling her face upwards, thus disguising wrinkles.

*Madame Medusa snaps into wakefulness as the very camp voice of **CRACK** comes over the speaker system.*

CRACK: *(O/S)* Madame Medusa, I've surely not caught you sleeping on the job!

MEDUSA: Oh don't.

CRACK: *(O/S)* Sweetheart, you've got to prepare yourself, you've got three this afternoon.

MEDUSA: Back to back?

CRACK: *(O/S)* 'Fraid so, one after the other, bang, bang, bang.

MEDUSA: You trying to be funny?

CRACK: *(O/S)* Would I?

MEDUSA: What time do you finish tonight?

CRACK: *(O/S)* Same as you.

MEDUSA: Fancy a drink?

CRACK: *(O/S)* Do I ever refuse?

MEDUSA: What's the camera situation?

CRACK: *(O/S)* Same as this morning shall we say? I think that means the drinks are on you... again!

Medusa laughs.

MEDUSA: You're a star.

CRACK: *(O/S)* And don't I know it. Twinkle, twinkle. See you later.

Medusa opens up a large form and begins to fill it in. There is a loud tuneful and playful knock at the door.

MEDUSA: Come in.

Medusa does not look up. **DEREK** *enters. He has a Latino lover style about him, everything is designed to emphasise raw sex, although his clothing also has a hint of a uniform about it. The belt around his trousers has a suggestive buckle. His boots are fancy.*

MEDUSA: Sit down.

DEREK: Here?

MEDUSA: There is only one chair.

DEREK: Two

He indicates her chair. As her head is still bent over the form she misses this.

MEDUSA: Only one spare chair.

DEREK: Just a joke.

Derek sits down.

MEDUSA: Name?

DEREK: Lothario.

MEDUSA: (*not looking up*) Real name?

DEREK: Lothario.

Medusa looks at him. Pause.

MEDUSA: The exit is that way.

She indicates stage left.

DEREK: But I was christened Derek.

MEDUSA: Thank you.

She writes this down.

Date of birth?

DEREK: Third of the eleventh. I'm a Scorpio.

MEDUSA: What year?

DEREK: 2018.

Medusa lays down her pen and leans back in her chair.

MEDUSA: You're too young then.

DEREK: No.

MEDUSA: Candidates have to be born 2006 at the latest. You obviously didn't read the application form properly.

DEREK: Yeah, but I'm a Scorpio.

MEDUSA: So are one twelfth of the male population.

DEREK: But it's well-known.

MEDUSA: What precisely?

DEREK: You know.

Medusa stands up.

MEDUSA: As I said, the exit is that way. Thank you.

He goes to leave.

DEREK: There is something else.

MEDUSA: There always is with your types.

DEREK: I've fathered three kids.

MEDUSA: Have you proof of that?

DEREK: Yeah.

MEDUSA: We'll continue.

She sits down and indicates to Derek to do the same.

MEDUSA: Which county were you born in?

DEREK: Cornwall.

MEDUSA: Really? Are you absolutely sure about that? Every male who comes through that door claims they were born in Cornwall since the article in the Sunday broadsheets.

DEREK: I really want the position.

MEDUSA: So does every male, to begin with.

DEREK: How do you mean?

MEDUSA: Which county?

DEREK: Hampshire.

MEDUSA: Any siblings?

DEREK: Three brothers.

MEDUSA: No sisters?

DEREK: Nope.

MEDUSA: Brothers all living?

DEREK: All alive and kicking.

MEDUSA: Dates of birth?

DEREK: Pass.

MEDUSA: Ages?

DEREK: Pass.

MEDUSA: It could have a bearing on your application.

DEREK: Barry's the eldest.

MEDUSA: Any of them fathers?

DEREK: This is meant to be questions about me.

MEDUSA: It is. Are they?

DEREK: Barry's got three kids and I've got three kids.

MEDUSA: So you said.

DEREK: I've got pictures of them.

MEDUSA: I'll photocopy them.

Derek begins to ferret in his jacket pocket.

You've done your sample?

DEREK: Yeah.

MEDUSA: Have you got the number?

DEREK: I'm just finding the photos first.

MEDUSA: Alright. What time did you give the sample?

DEREK: Just before I came in here.

MEDUSA: You did the sample on the premises?

DEREK: Yeah. Here.

He shows her the photos.

This is Benjy, Markie and Carl.

MEDUSA: Ages?

DEREK: Ten, five and two.

MEDUSA: Same mother?

DEREK: (*proudly*) No. Three different mothers.

MEDUSA: Really? So you were twenty-one when you fathered the eldest, twenty nine with the youngest. Do you have any further proof with you?

DEREK: You can see we all look alike.

MEDUSA: No, I can't see that. I'll need birth certificates for each of them.

DEREK: How do I get hold of them?

MEDUSA: You don't have copies?

DEREK: No.

MEDUSA: The mothers will, it's the law.

DEREK: I don't want to contact the mothers!

MEDUSA: I'm afraid you have no choice if you wish to pursue your application.

There is a strained silence.

DEREK: I only know where two of them are.

MEDUSA: Which child do I need to discount?

DEREK: But I've got three.

MEDUSA: You can only prove two.

DEREK: The youngest, Carl.

MEDUSA: For the application form then, you fathered your last child when you were twenty six?

DEREK: This isn't fair.

MEDUSA: Every male has the same criteria, it is as fair as we can make it.

DEREK: When do I need to bring the birth certificates in?

MEDUSA: Let's not jump the gun. We haven't finished the rest of the form. You may not be suitable.

DEREK: I heard you were desperate.

MEDUSA: Only for the right candidates. Specimen number?

Derek hands her a form.

Thank you.

Medusa transfers the details.

MEDUSA: Have you ever applied here before?

DEREK: No.

MEDUSA: Have you ever applied at other Centrals?

DEREK: No.

MEDUSA: We will be cross referencing.

DEREK: No, never.

MEDUSA: I need to go back. The other brothers, are they fathers?

DEREK: We all are.

MEDUSA: Really? Right, John, how many children?

DEREK: Two boys.

MEDUSA: Male or female?

DEREK: We've all got boys.

MEDUSA: Stevie has how many boys?

DEREK: Four.

MEDUSA: Are you sure?

DEREK: He is my brother.

MEDUSA: So between you, you have apparently fathered twelve children?

DEREK: Yeah.

MEDUSA: Are you aware of how unusual that is in this climate? Have they been seen by Central?

DEREK: Dunno.

MEDUSA: We'd be very interested in interviewing them if they haven't.

DEREK: Err... That's why I'm here.

MEDUSA: Why haven't you applied before?

DEREK: It's not compulsory.

MEDUSA: Yet.

DEREK: I wanted a little fun before I did my duty to my country.

He laughs. Medusa puts her pen down and looks at him.

MEDUSA: What have you heard about this job?

DEREK: It's well paid.

MEDUSA: Is it?

DEREK: Yeah, for what it is.

MEDUSA: I see.

DEREK: Accommodation is good. Per diems are good.

MEDUSA: And where did you glean all this information?

DEREK: Two mates of mine have done it.

MEDUSA: Unlikely.

DEREK: Straight up. Oh, bad joke.

MEDUSA: Innuendo always appears to be rife at the interview stage.

DEREK: Anyway they said it was an ace job with all the trimmings.

MEDUSA: How long did they work for Central?

DEREK: 'Bout six months I think.

MEDUSA: Even more unlikely.

DEREK: They wouldn't lie.

MEDUSA: Why ever not?

DEREK: They're mates.

MEDUSA: How charmingly simplistic.

DEREK: I don't lie, so why should they?

MEDUSA: No reason at all, Lothario.

DEREK: That was just a joke!

MEDUSA: Perhaps your friends make jokes, too.

DEREK: Look...

MEDUSA: In fact if you have their names I can check for you right away.

DEREK: I only know their nicknames.

MEDUSA: No good then. Do you know which division they supposedly worked in?

DEREK: Don't know what you mean?

MEDUSA: Ah, something you don't know about the position you've applied for.

DEREK: Stands to reason women are just women.

MEDUSA: Divisions are dictated by the age of the women.

DEREK: I'll have the sixteen to twenty division if there's a choice going.

MEDUSA: It doesn't work like that. It depends on the activity of your sample.

DEREK: My boys are all fighters.

MEDUSA: The analysis will tell us whether that is the case or not. If your sample shows great activity you will be placed in the older female division, forty to forty eight.

DEREK: No, I couldn't, that'd be like screwing my mum.

MEDUSA: Can I remind you that you are applying for a job not a holiday. Again if your sample is very active you will alternate with the youngest division.

DEREK: Now you're talking.

MEDUSA: They are all from menstruating age.

DEREK: What's that?

MEDUSA: Menstruating?

DEREK: I'm not that thick. What age?

MEDUSA: Ten to fourteen.

DEREK: No, I'm not screwing kids! That would have been against the law forty years ago!

MEDUSA: Yes.

DEREK: That's not normal.

MEDUSA: What is normal anymore?

DEREK: Look, I could just about manage the old hags, but I'm not doing kids.

MEDUSA: Choices are not part of the contract.

DEREK: How would you feel?

MEDUSA: It's not my job to feel.

DEREK: If it was your daughter?

MEDUSA: I don't have a daughter.

DEREK: A son?

MEDUSA: Is this dealing with your application? No. To continue, if you are successful in applying for the job, you will have to accept the terms of the contract.

DEREK: Can I see one?

MEDUSA: Can you read?

DEREK: A bit.

MEDUSA: Here.

She passes him a contract. Derek cannot read very well but makes a valiant effort.

DEREK: What are the hours?

MEDUSA: They're explained in point 2.4.

DEREK: Just tell me then.

MEDUSA: Hours are changeable due to the optimum fertility highs of the individual women that you will be servicing.

DEREK: Servicing?

MEDUSA: That's the terminology that is used.

DEREK: It means screwing though, doesn't it?

MEDUSA: I think you will use the term servicing after the first week.

DEREK: How many do I have to 'service' a day then?

MEDUSA: Again depending on the activity within your sample and your recovery rate –

DEREK: Ten minutes max.

MEDUSA: - in order to bring your sample back up to full activity, anything between ten to fifteen women per day.

DEREK: (*delightedly*) Oh what! Is it like in eight hour shifts?

MEDUSA: As I said previously, it is dependent on the woman's optimum fertility times.

DEREK: Meaning?

MEDUSA: That you are on call twenty four hours a day. Four days on two days off.

DEREK: I won't need that long off.

Medusa sighs.

MEDUSA: Do you smoke?

DEREK: Now and again.

MEDUSA: Smoking is strictly prohibited for obvious reasons. Recreational drugs?

DEREK: Bit of dope, that's about it.

MEDUSA: Dope is also prohibited, however a limited supply of cocaine will be given to you every twenty four hours to use at your leisure.

DEREK: Great. Booze?

MEDUSA: The women are allowed two glasses of wine per day, men are not allowed alcohol.

DEREK: That's not fair.

MEDUSA: It has been proved that female libido can be enhanced with a moderate amount of alcohol to relax them prior to sex. On the contrary it can deplete a man's.

DEREK: Not me sweetheart.

MEDUSA: I'm going to make a suggestion, if you wish your application to be successful do not call me sweetheart.

DEREK: Sorry.

MEDUSA: Have you got your medical certificate?

DEREK: Yeah.

He hands it over to Medusa, she looks at it and fills in a few parts of her form.

MEDUSA: You will of course have to have a thorough medical should your application be accepted.

DEREK: No problem.

MEDUSA: We'll be contacting your Health Centre.

DEREK: What for?

MEDUSA: To cross-reference.

DEREK: Why, don't you trust me?

MEDUSA: It's procedure. We cross-reference all new applicants.

DEREK: Well, you don't have to with me.

MEDUSA: It's standard procedure.

DEREK: I don't get this.

There is a Silence.

I'm applying for a job of screwing, that's all, why all the Gestapo stuff? I mean how desperate are you? I don't know why I'm bothering. I mean I can have it away any day of the week if I want. Just thought I'd do the country a favour, do my duty for a while in a bit of comfort!

MEDUSA: Temper tantrums don't tend to aid applications, on the whole.

DEREK: Fuck you! I'm going.

Derek pushes his chair back roughly and moves to the door.

MEDUSA: I assume from your outburst (she waves the medical certificate at him) this isn't worth the paper it's written on?

DEREK: Piss off.

Derek reaches the door to discover that he cannot open it.

Bloody door's jammed.

MEDUSA: Locked.

DEREK: Yeah, pull the other one.

Derek tries the door again, it doesn't budge.

MEDUSA: I suggest we continue.

DEREK: Right, enough, get this door opened, now.

MEDUSA: Or?

DEREK: I'll do something we'll both regret.

Medusa grins to herself.

MEDUSA: Where did you obtain this Medical Certificate?

DEREK: From my Health Centre, where do you think? Now get this door open, I'm getting wound up here!

MEDUSA: I can't do that.

Derek moves towards her threateningly.

DEREK: Get the sodding door opened!

MEDUSA: Beyond my power I'm afraid. Once you enter an interview room the doors are automatically locked by Security until the interview is concluded and more importantly that your sample has been tested.

DEREK: You can't do that.

MEDUSA: We live in desperate times Derek.

DEREK: I'm imprisoned.

MEDUSA: Only temporarily.

DEREK: When do I get out of here?

MEDUSA: From this actual room?

DEREK: Yeah.

MEDUSA: I've told you.

DEREK: Yeah, but how long is that going to be?

MEDUSA: It all depends.

DEREK: On what?

MEDUSA: How quickly we complete the interview and how busy the labs are.

DEREK: (*shouting*) For fucks sake! I can't cope with being cooped up! Open the fucking door!

Silence. Derek suddenly makes a lunge at Medusa. She dodges swiftly and silently. Derek misjudging, ends up on the floor, face down. By this time Medusa has produced what looks like a gun. Derek rolls onto his back and sees it.

DEREK: Hey!

MEDUSA: We need to continue with the interview.

DEREK: Look, sorry. OK, I'll sit down again.

MEDUSA: I suggest you move very, very slowly.

DEREK: OK. OK.

Derek does as he's told and moves back to his chair. Medusa has the gun trained on him the whole time. Once he has sat down she puts the gun back inside her uniform.

MEDUSA: Picking up where we left off, the Medical Certificate.

DEREK: Would you have shot me?

MEDUSA: If necessary.

DEREK: Killed me?

MEDUSA: Unlikely with a stun gun. Medical Certificate, where did you get it?

DEREK: I paid for it, on the black market. A stun gun?

MEDUSA: Yes. Was it from one of the following establishments?

She reads from a laminated list in her folder

Charlie's Bar, Mega-Market, Celan, Roger's Restaurant or Roger's Enterprises?

DEREK: Charlie's Bar.

MEDUSA: How much?

DEREK: Can't remember.

Medusa looks at him.

Three hundred and fifty. Where would you have shot me?

MEDUSA: We're trained to hit the upper arm or thighs. Euros?

DEREK: Yeah.

MEDUSA: You should have gone to Roger, he's much cheaper.

DEREK: Great, thanks. I'll know for next time. Have you shot other blokes?

MEDUSA: Once or twice.

DEREK: It's a bit drastic, isn't it?

MEDUSA: I don't think so.

DEREK: I mean we're only applying for a job.

MEDUSA: It is probably the most important job in the world.

DEREK: Watch it, my head'll begin to swell.

MEDUSA: You haven't got it yet.

DEREK: No, but I bet I will.

MEDUSA: We tend to be very selective.

DEREK: Bollocks. You might be selective with the birds, but basically if the bloke's got fighter pilots you'll take him, won't you?

MEDUSA: Not necessarily.

DEREK: Look, there's more and more blokes firing blanks. Any bloke that's firing a fighter has got to be in with a chance.

MEDUSA: Our interview process...

DEREK: Means bugger all if the bloke has got working jizz.

MEDUSA: It is not that simple!

DEREK: Oh, who rattled your cage?

Medusa is furious with herself for showing her feelings. And desperately tries to compose herself.

MEDUSA: I need to ask you some further questions.

Medusa goes back to the form.

>Where did you hear about us?

DEREK: I want to carry on discussing the selection process.

MEDUSA: Where did you hear about us?

DEREK: Everyone knows about Centrals.

MEDUSA: This particular Central.

DEREK: Local paper I think.

MEDUSA: Which is?

DEREK: Jissom Journal.

Medusa looks at him.

Word of mouth.

MEDUSA: When you say everyone knows about Centrals, could you clarify that for me?

DEREK: What's to clarify?

MEDUSA: Who's everyone?

DEREK: Well, everyone.

MEDUSA: Brothers, sisters, cousins twice removed?

DEREK: Mates.

MEDUSA: So mainly your male friends?

DEREK: Suppose so.

Medusa writes this down.

MEDUSA: Have any of these 'mates' applied for an interview?

DEREK: Dunno. It's not the sort of thing you talk about, is it?

MEDUSA: Why not?

DEREK: You know.

MEDUSA: If I knew, I wouldn't waste my breath asking.

DEREK: I don't want my mates knowing I'm going to get paid for sex.

MEDUSA: This is for your country, not merely for your pocket.

DEREK: Yeah, but at the end of the day, you're still getting paid for having sex with a woman. Don't want people calling me a gigolo.

MEDUSA: We don't use the word sex, we use the term Fertility Fighting.

DEREK: Give me a break, fertility fighting? (*he laughs*) Dress it up as much as you like, it's still just sex I'm getting paid for.

MEDUSA: Then why have you applied?

DEREK: 'Cos I personally don't mind being paid for screwing, for my country, so long as nobody else knows about it.

MEDUSA: These women are specially selected to be part of the Government Fertility Programme. If a pregnancy occurs it's considered a high achievement for the man and the woman.

DEREK: Good. (*pause*) Is that the right response?

MEDUSA: What about your 'mates' who claim to have worked here before? Do you view them as gigolos?

DEREK: Yeah, but this is the only place those ugly bastards are guaranteed sex.

Medusa shakes her head in disbelief and returns to the form.

MEDUSA: Have you ever donated your sperm to any Insemination Centres?

DEREK: My boys in a test-tube? Leave it out, I'm a bit fussy, got my pride. Wouldn't want them ending up inside any old cow.

MEDUSA: Do not refer to the women as cows.

DEREK: Dogs then.

MEDUSA: If you carry on in this vein I can almost guarantee that your application will fail.

DEREK: Oh?

Medusa looks at him. He leans forward.

I think, until the lab results come back, you're on shaky ground coming out with a statement like that.

Medusa tries to stare him down unsuccessfully and eventually has to retreat back to the form.

MEDUSA: Have you ever been a member of any religious groups purporting the taking of more than one wife?

DEREK: No. Never been married.

MEDUSA: Have you ever donated sperm to an IVF Unit?

DEREK: No, 'cos they don't pay.

MEDUSA: Moving on. Have you seen the Central tables of success?

DEREK: No.

MEDUSA: Would you be interested in hearing the tables of success?

DEREK: Not particularly.

MEDUSA: It is part of my duty within this interview to inform you of the tables of success.

DEREK: Sorry, you should have said. I mean I'd hate to be the one that stopped you doing your duty, *hofficer*.

He does a mock salute.

MEDUSA: At present we are running at an overall success rate of 2%.

DEREK: 2%? That's pathetic.

MEDUSA: It's average.

DEREK: How many women?

MEDUSA: It's kept at one hundred.

DEREK: How the bloody hell are you selecting them?

MEDUSA: Scientifically.

DEREK: Not working, is it?

MEDUSA: You have a better method?

DEREK: No, no. (*pause*) Have you been interviewed? Scientifically, you know.

He winks lewdly and Medusa pulls out the stun gun.

DEREK: Hey, I'm just asking.

MEDUSA: No.

Pause.

DEREK: You have, haven't you? You've been scientifically rejected!

He finds this very funny, laughs again then stops abruptly.

How old are you?

Pause.

You don't have to answer anything, I'm just curious. I'd say you're about – forty-four?

Medusa is chuffed despite her better judgement.

MEDUSA: Almost.

DEREK: Go on, was I right?

MEDUSA: A little older.

DEREK: Had a face lift?

Medusa realises that she's been caught in his trap.

MEDUSA: I... I...

DEREK: Thought so. Don't know a woman over thirty-five who hasn't these days.

Was it expensive?

There is a Silence.

Thing is a face lift doesn't make you fertile, does it? When are women going to realise that? I suppose they do it to try to catch a more virile man. Like me.

(*pause*) Is that why you did it? (*pause*) Have you had one of these womb lifts too?

Medusa shifts uncomfortably.

Oh dear. Now I know that they're expensive and not very reliable by all accounts.

MEDUSA: If you carry on like this, I'll call Security.

DEREK: How?

MEDUSA: What?

DEREK: How will you call Security? There's no phone. (he looks around) No cameras.

MEDUSA: The cameras are hidden.

DEREK: Oh right. In that case, why didn't Security leg it in here when I had a go at you?

Medusa is floundering.

MEDUSA: They know that I'm trained to look after myself. But if you persist in this manner –

DEREK: What manner? We're just having a conversation.

MEDUSA: - you'll leave me no alternative but to use the stun gun.

DEREK: Oh, how terrifying.

Medusa picks up the stun gun, Derek stands up.

Go on then, in the thigh.

MEDUSA: I mean it.

DEREK: So do I. I could do with a few hours kip.

There is a Silence.

MEDUSA: I don't like your attitude.

DEREK: Shame.

MEDUSA: You're treating this whole thing as a joke.

DEREK: No, that's unfair. It's just it's the easiest job I've ever applied for.

MEDUSA: Is it really?

DEREK: Well I know I've got the right equipment for the job in hand. Want to test me out? Ride the goods?

MEDUSA: I…

DEREK: Don't be too hasty. Give yourself a bit of time to think about my offer.

MEDUSA: You're forgetting something. I see the men before, during and after their time here.

DEREK: And?

MEDUSA: I've made the observation that you're all the same. You all come in preening at the interview, thinking you're God's gift.

DEREK: Your words not mine, but I'll take it as a compliment.

MEDUSA: That's what I mean, cocky.

DEREK: Hope so for a job like this.

MEDUSA: And after the first week's work, it's a completely different story.

DEREK: Really?

MEDUSA: Yes, because the cockiness gets pumped out of you. You all end up complaining you can't perform, you're not animals. And suddenly the penny drops and you macho men realise it's a job. A hard job. And none of you, not one of you so far has been up to it.

DEREK: Perhaps I'm the one to break the mould.

MEDUSA: I doubt it.

DEREK: Bet you'd like to find out though.

MEDUSA: You're not the first applicant who's tried it on, you know.

DEREK: You're an attractive woman, what man wouldn't want to jump you? A beautiful, curvaceous feminine woman, come on!

Medusa lowers her head.

Genuinely. Are you blushing? That's lovely, a woman who can still blush.

MEDUSA: I'm not blushing.

DEREK: Hey, it's great to see a woman who can still be feminine.

Medusa looks at him in surprise.

Do you like old movies?

MEDUSA: I don't watch much television.

DEREK: That wasn't the question.

MEDUSA: Some.

DEREK: I love them. Nineteen thirties, forties, seeing women as they used to be. Soft, vulnerable, needing protection.

MEDUSA: Women who are totally suppressed?

DEREK: You don't think it was part of the balance of nature? And that's why women aren't getting pregnant now?

MEDUSA: No, it's because of manufactured oestrogen in the food chain, water pollution, plastics, reactive tinned food, you hear the news.

DEREK: Those are all outside things, what about the inside things?

MEDUSA: They're the scientifically proven facts.

DEREK: Look, I'm not talking about the right and wrong of it, suppression and all that. I'm talking about just the way it was. Women didn't go out doing all the grafting, they stayed at home, getting round and broody. Men went out and grafted and came home hard and horny.

MEDUSA: (*sarcastically*) So by your definition is: working women equals loss of fertility?

DEREK: No, it's that, plus men losing their grafting drive which means they're no longer producing the goods.

MEDUSA: Sperm?

DEREK: My sex have been emasculated. They're all house husbands, doing admin, cooking, knitting, sewing. Everything's been tipped on its head.

MEDUSA: Doesn't your success rate as a father put a hole in that argument?

DEREK: Firstly, I've never let a woman look after me financially. Point two, I never go for high-powered women. Although for you I might make an exception. Point three, when I'm with a woman I look after her.

MEDUSA: Financially?

DEREK: Every which way! Financially, romantically. I make the big decisions about life so that she doesn't have to worry about anything.

MEDUSA: And women actually let you do that?

DEREK: They love it. And it redresses the balance, it makes for fertility again.

MEDUSA: If you're so sure about your theories and the fact that they work, why haven't you gone to the government with them?

DEREK: Why should I?

MEDUSA: Because the human race is dying out!

DEREK: No. There are babies being born, all the time. It's just that they're not always recorded.

MEDUSA: But the law commands –

DEREK: The law does command, but not everybody is a good boy. What if we did go like good little citizens and record every birth, what would they do?

MEDUSA: Use the information to help mankind.

DEREK: No. They'd start analysing and testing and doing all the things that happen here. They'd take all the spark out of it.

MEDUSA: If you feel like that why have you applied for the job?

DEREK: I want to see what it's like.

MEDUSA: I don't believe you.

DEREK: You don't have to.

MEDUSA: So running your theory, if I gave my job up, met a man or men who looked after me, I could become pregnant?

DEREK: Man, not men. And yes.

MEDUSA: You're a fool.

DEREK: Am I?

MEDUSA: A very confident fool.

DEREK: And you are intrigued. I can see you questioning yourself.

Medusa looks at him intently.

MEDUSA: With your... beliefs, you'd hate this job.

DEREK: I don't think so. I love sex.

MEDUSA: None of the men like it.

DEREK: Probably not real men.

MEDUSA: They all think they are.

DEREK: Have you been with a real man?

MEDUSA: I think we need to continue with the interview.

DEREK: Do we? I'm enjoying the chat.

MEDUSA: I'm here to work not socialise.

DEREK: You could break the rules. Or are you too scared?

MEDUSA: I'm scared of very little.

DEREK: What about me?

Pause. She pushes the paperwork aside very deliberately.

MEDUSA: Do you have a girlfriend?

DEREK: 'Til two months ago.

MEDUSA: I didn't mean to pry.

DEREK: I don't mind. Ask away.

MEDUSA: Why did it end?

DEREK: She caved in and decided to get a job. Getting a load of pressure from her mum and her gran about not being a corporate girl. No choice but to stick to my principles and end it.

MEDUSA: Did she want that?

DEREK: 'Course not, but I told you, I don't want to be with a high-flier. You got anybody?

MEDUSA: No.

DEREK: We're both free then.

MEDUSA: Yes.

Pause.

DEREK: How long have you been on your own?

MEDUSA: A while.

DEREK: Who finished with who?

MEDUSA: He finished with me.

DEREK: What a fool. Sad.

MEDUSA: He wanted a child.

DEREK: Ah.

MEDUSA: We'd been trying for years. He felt that perhaps a younger woman would be a better bet. I don't blame him.

DEREK: Did he live off you?

MEDUSA: I bought the money in, if that's what you mean.

DEREK: Does he live off this new one?

MEDUSA: Yes, of course. It's the way of the world.

DEREK: I rest my case. Do you want a baby?

MEDUSA: What woman doesn't?

DEREK: I'm worth a try.

MEDUSA: What?

DEREK: I could give you a baby.

MEDUSA: You're an applicant, I can't be serviced by an applicant!

DEREK: I don't want to service you. I want to have sex with you!

Medusa laughs.

MEDUSA: Is that your chat up line?

DEREK: No. I would like to lay you.

MEDUSA: That's a disgusting expression.

DEREK: Is it? Wouldn't you like to be laid by me? Lots of women do.

MEDUSA: I have standards.

DEREK: So Do I.

MEDUSA: Does it move, is it female?

DEREK: You are in need of some serious loving.

MEDUSA: And you are in need of brain surgery.

Pause.

DEREK: How long do they take to test a sample?

MEDUSA: You do know that if your sample is good, you won't be going home?

DEREK: Oh?

MEDUSA: I'm not trying to be confrontational, just telling you how it is. There are such a shortage of men with decent sperm counts, you're too precious to let go. You'll be taken straight to the stables.

DEREK: The stables?

He laughs.

MEDUSA: Yes, it's where the servicing takes place.

DEREK: The servicing of the women takes place in the stables, m'lud. No wonder there's only a 2% success rate here. Where's the lust, the love, the romance?

MEDUSA: Why have you really applied?

DEREK: Curiosity, that's all.

MEDUSA: They'll keep you here indefinitely, until they've milked you dry.

DEREK: Very funny, I'll just stop performing.

MEDUSA: They won't let you.

DEREK: How can they stop me?

MEDUSA: Non-performers are put into solitary.

DEREK: That's not going help much is it?

MEDUSA: Solitary means you're placed in a small cubicle with a large screen playing hardcore movies twenty-four hours a day. Most men cannot help responding to visual and aural stimuli, it's usually only a matter of hours before they are ready again. The longest a man has stayed in solitary is three days, but then it was discovered he had a virus.

DEREK: You're joking.

MEDUSA: No.

DEREK: It's worse than I thought.

MEDUSA: You would hate it.

DEREK: Why are you telling me this?

MEDUSA: I've no idea.

DEREK: I mean, I can't escape, can I? The door's locked, and according to you, I'm going to be kidnapped when my sample comes back.

Pause.

> I wonder, can you get out of this room?

Medusa stays silent.

> Do I have to beat the secret out of you?

Medusa smiles.

> No, you'd get me with your stun gun. Do I have to beg it out of you? No, I don't think that's what you'd want either. (*Pause*) Do I have to screw it out of you?

Medusa bows her head.

> You realise you're asking me to break my own rules?

MEDUSA: What do you mean?

DEREK: Laying a high-flier.

MEDUSA: I suppose it depends how strong your principles are and how much you want to get out of here before you're trapped. And time must be running out.

DEREK: What about the Security cameras?

MEDUSA: We could switch the lights off.

DEREK: Won't that make them suspicious?

MEDUSA: I shouldn't think so.

DEREK: (*slowly*) You shouldn't think so?

MEDUSA: I'm not lying.

DEREK: If you want my boys pumping up inside you, you'd better start being straight with me, right now.

MEDUSA: Look, I don't make a habit of this.

DEREK: Screwing the applicants?

MEDUSA: Yeah, but there aren't many perks to this job.

DEREK: And when a good opportunity comes your way...

MEDUSA: Something like that.

DEREK: Are you allowed to do that?

MEDUSA: What do you think?

DEREK: Are you fertile now?

MEDUSA: Yes, eleventh day.

DEREK: Have you been with anybody else today?

MEDUSA: No, you're my first applicant.

DEREK: Ok. I'll do it.

MEDUSA: We'll have to be quick.

DEREK: Pity, I'd have liked the chance to spend a long time over you.

Derek begins to unbutton his shirt.

MEDUSA: You don't need to take your shirt off!

DEREK: That quick?

Medusa puts the light out, Derek unzips himself pushes her against the table.

DEREK: Against the table, spread your legs.

MEDUSA: Isn't it easier if I sit on you?

DEREK: How many times have you done this?

MEDUSA: No, I just thought it might be easier.

DEREK: Against the table, quickly.

MEDUSA: Ow.

DEREK: Sorry, sorry, you alright?

MEDUSA: The table was digging into me.

DEREK: Hold your skirt up. Yeah, I'm in, ah, oh.

The unpleasant sound of Derek grunting is all that can be heard, screws her, comes really quickly.

Oh yeah. Um-um Derek does it again.

MEDUSA: Finished already?

DEREK: Yeah.

MEDUSA: You did come didn't you?

DEREK: You must have felt it?

MEDUSA: Yeah, sorry. Can you put the light on?

Derek zips himself up and goes to put the light on as Medusa rearranges her skirt. He is grinning like a Cheshire cat. Medusa has moved back to her chair and puts her feet on the table. Derek looks at her questioningly.

>Apparently there's more chance if you have your feet higher than your head for five minutes afterwards.

DEREK: Old wives tale.

MEDUSA: Got to be worth a try though.

DEREK: No, depends entirely on the male's sperm strength.

MEDUSA: I didn't know that.

Sound of a speaker system crackling into life.

CRACK: *(O/S)* Room 7, red alert, red alert, abort interview with immediate affect, repeat, abort interview with immediate affect.

Medusa looks stunned and removes her feet from the table.

DEREK: Is that us by any chance?

MEDUSA: That can't be right.

DEREK: Well, I have been in here over half an hour.

MEDUSA: But that message means...

Medusa stares at Derek with a slow dawning. Derek starts to back towards the door.

> Get out, you liar, you bloody liar! Get out.

DEREK: Hey, hey, I showed you a good time? Where's your manners?

MEDUSA: You lied to me, you bastard, you bastard!

She begins to hit at him, Derek opens the door and is heard laughing as he exits.

DEREK: You were ready to believe anything darling. You've only got yourself to blame. Madame Medusa, the bike, you're called on the outside. Madame Medusa, the bike!

Medusa is left helpless in the room knowing she is the only person to blame for her predicament.

CRACK: (*O/S*) Win some lose some ducky! Two more to go and I'll tell you what, the drinks will be on me!

Blackout

End of Play